HORSE SENSE

The Essential Humorous Guide
for Parents and Riders

GW00707451

HORSE SENSE
The Essential Humorous Guide for Parents and Riders

Jennifer Hart

JANUS PUBLISHING COMPANY
London, England

First published in Great Britain 1996
by Janus Publishing Company,
Edinburgh House, 19 Nassau Street,
London W1N 7RE

Copyright © Jennifer Hart 1996

British Library Cataloguing-in-Publication Data.
A catalogue record for this book is available from the
British Library.

ISBN 1 85756 211 9

Cover design Linda Wade

Printed & bound in England by
Antony Rowe Ltd,
Chippenham, Wiltshire

INTRODUCTION

NO ONE TO BLAME
BUT OURSELVES

In the beginning, when God (or Mother Nature, depending on your religious or sexist beliefs) created the horse, he or she got things about right. The first horse, Eohippus, was a charming little creature about the size of a fox, with a brain in perfect proportion to its body. It did no harm to anyone and, indeed, helped many other creatures on the planet by acting as lunch, dinner and tea. It was a much-hunted animal, with eyes positioned to the side of its dainty head to enable it to keep a look out for predators. Now, if things had only stayed that way we would probably all be a lot better off. However, as the earth started to warm up and vegetation became more plentiful, so the horse began to grow.

Well, I say the horse began to grow, but the sad truth is that only certain parts grew and they were the dangerous bits. As a fox-like animal, Eohippus had five small toes on the end of scrawny legs, making it very nimble. By the time the horse had grown into the type of animal we know today, its legs had become longer and thicker and those toes had fused together to create one large, very hard hoof. Dog-sized teeth grew into awesome munchers and its body grew to an enormous bulk.

But the real tragedy of this depressing tail (sorry, tale) is that the horse's brain stayed exactly the same size! Today the horse is one of the most beautiful, graceful and powerful creatures on earth – but it has a brain the size of a grapefruit! It doesn't take the mind of an Einstein to work out that this is a potentially explosive situation, but unfortunately it doesn't end there. There is one more small fly in the ointment.

Surprisingly, this fly is man. 'What is surprising about that?' I hear you cry. Well, normally man has a very strong sense of self-preservation, but in this case he seems to have made a very serious error of judgement which has probably affected the very foundations of civilisation as we know it; he domesticated the horse! He bred them to be bigger, faster and stronger, selecting the best specimens to keep and leaving the smaller ponies to run wild. This is where we get so many of our native ponies from. They were the ones originally turned loose on the moors because man initially thought that they were too small to be of any use. And as if those huge feet weren't dangerous enough, what does man do next? He nails great big chunks of metal to the bottom of them to protect them from wear and tear. His next trick is to confine this wild animal, which is used to having miles of open space to wander around in, to a small box, simply for his own convenience. Are these the rational actions of sane people?

Well, to give them the benefit of the doubt, perhaps they didn't realise the trouble they were letting themselves in for until it was too late. Because, let's face it, until recently, by evolutionary standards, the horse had been reasonably useful. The larger versions had carried our medieval ancestors into battle, pulled carriages for transport and

The Horse became somewhat redundant!

ploughs on the farm, and even the smaller varieties had made excellent pack animals. The pit ponies, with their incredible strength-to-size ratio, will go down in industrial history for ever. But the invention of tanks, cars, lorries and tractors meant that the horse became somewhat redundant.

So what on earth are we supposed to do with it now? I personally can't work out why man had to interfere in the first place, but we have to accept that everyone makes mistakes and the main thing is to try to learn from them. However, now that we have inherited these obsolete workers, we seem to be oblivious to the follies of our fore-bears and are simply compounding the problem by keeping them for sport (I've always suspected that man has a sick sense of humour) and, even more unbelievably, as pets for our children! Now, that is like giving the poor infant a boa constrictor, only with a higher risk factor. Boa constrictors only crush things. Horses bite, kick and run off, usually dragging some unfortunate youngster (or adult) behind them and just when you think the worst is over, then crush things. You are not safe on top either, as they will try their hardest to get you off and, when they have succeeded, will then run away.

Don't get me wrong, I would not dream of getting rid of these creatures, I just find it hard to comprehend the fanatical following that they have acquired. If any pop group could muster the same degree of interest, they would be made for life. Horses are currently making the biggest comeback in popularity since Frank Sinatra, but one has to wonder if people really understand what they are taking on when they buy one of their own. It is all very well riding at the local stables once a week, but taking full responsibility for the care of a horse or pony is considerably different from hiring one by the hour.

I have no sympathy at all for the adults who knowingly saddle themselves with one of these animals and, funnily enough, very little for the children who become enchanted by the beasts. These people seem to be either reasonably well informed about the behavioural characteristics of their idols or selectively blind to their faults. My very deep sympathies lie with the members of our society who, through total ignorance, allow themselves to be cajoled or browbeaten into buying one – the parents. It is to those poor, misguided, albeit well-meaning individuals that I dedicate this book, although the advice and observations contained in it may be of equal interest to anyone considering embarking on the path to mental and financial ruin.

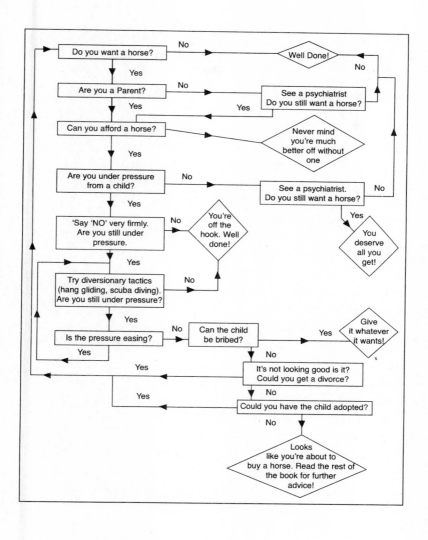

PART ONE

DEAR
MR BANK MANAGER

My first piece of advice to any parent whose darling off-spring asks for a pony or horse of their very own is: say NO! You may have been foolish enough to allow your child to start riding, but surely you cannot possibly have been so naive as to believe this question would not arise. After all, doesn't the man who takes up golf want his own set of clubs or the child who has piano lessons want their own baby grand? It is the very unfortunate but natural progression of things.

When your beloved child does utter those fateful words, under no circumstances should you say 'I'll think about it'. That is cruel both to yourself and the child. You must be firm and determined, even when the subject is raised on a daily or even hourly basis. Young Alice or Oliver will have their hopes raised and you will not get a single minute's peace until you finally crack. Anyone who has heard a child going on and on and on until they get what they want will know that it is a bit like the Chinese Water Torture; it wears you down eventually.

One of the easiest ways of avoiding the question ever

arising is quite simply not to let them go riding in the first place. This is all very well for me to say, with the benefit of hindsight, and I realise that for many of you this statement comes a little too late. But do not be too downhearted; there are several very good ways of diverting their attention away from the stables. Take them hang gliding or deep sea diving, anything that is dangerous and exciting and very time-consuming. Motor racing is another high risk sport that offers opportunities for competition if that is what they want and, although expensive, a racing car doesn't have the same physical needs as a pony.

Those of you who aren't parents (henceforth known as LOWMS – Lucky Ones With More Sense) should ask yourselves just why you want a horse. Wouldn't you rather go hang gliding, deep sea diving or even, if you want to do something really reckless, have children instead? If the answer to any or all of these questions is no, then may I suggest you try a good psychiatrist or hypnotist and find out exactly what it is that is making you feel so hell-bent on self-destruction?

If at the end of the day, however, your little dear has a particularly appealing face (or owns a set of thumbscrews), or your psychiatrist has written you off as a totally incurable case, and you should happen to decide to look into the possibilities of such a foolish move, I feel that it is my moral obligation to let you in on some of the pitfalls so that you cannot say that you weren't warned.

The main consideration is where you are going to keep your horse. Questions like, 'How the hell am I going to be able to afford it?' are extremely trivial and will not be dealt with here. That is a matter for you and your bank manager to fall out over. The back garden will not do unless it happens to be over an acre in size and you don't like flowers. If it is more than an acre, can be grassed over and you don't mind thousands of flies round the house in the summer, keeping your pony at home will at least mean that you are always on hand if the rest of your family need your attention. But any stables that you erect will need planning permission and your neighbours might not be quite so keen on the idea. If you do choose stabling for your horse, do not let anyone other than a professional builder construct it. Go to a firm that specialises in building stables, otherwise (particularly if your 'man around the house' is as useless at DIY as mine) you could find that the first good kick will have it in a heap on the floor. If you don't have room at home, any field that you may have access to will need fencing secure enough to put Fort Knox to shame. If there is a way out, no matter how improbable you think it is, Houdini Horse will find it.

Houdini Horse

I can assure you that it is not very pleasant to be woken up at three o'clock in the morning by your local constabulary, wanting to know if you are responsible for the little fat pony that is currently playing with the traffic on the bypass. They are masters of the art of escapology, especially the little ones. It is worth making the point here that the smaller ponies tend to be the cleverest. I believe it has something to do with the fact that the less body there is to be controlled, the more it can use its minute brain for devious, underhand thinking purposes.

Although pasture maintenance can be a very technical and scientific subject which needs a great deal of study and careful planning if it is to be done effectively, it is often easier (for the human side of the deal anyway) to keep your horse in a field. At least that way you can hopefully borrow your friendly neighbourhood farmer's tractor and harrow and just spread the muck about a bit every now and again, thus saving on the back-breaking mucking out. If he won't lend you his tractor, he might just lend you the harrow, in which case you can make the kids pull it up and down the field. It might also make you feel a bit better if you walk behind them cracking a whip. I believe revenge can be very therapeutic.

If you can't find a suitable field, or your horse starts sneezing and shivering at the very mention of the word 'outside', keeping him in a stable is your only other option. But it is here that the word 'domesticated' comes into dispute. This would suggest that the horse is a clean and tidy animal but this, as you will soon find to your cost, this very definitely is not the case. A healthy horse passes up to eight piles of ready-made manure a day (more if he has got a dodgy tummy) and you are expected to clean it all up after him. Don't listen to the child who says that they will do all that. They will, until the novelty wears off or it gets too cold and dark for them to venture out in the winter. They won't want to do it too often in the summer either, when all their friends are going swimming and having fun. You will be lumbered with all the responsibility but none of the glory, and not only are horses dangerous – they smell!

The Domesticated Horse!
There's no such thing!

Horse odour is an intrusive smell; that means it gets into everything – your house, your car, your clothes and, no matter how often you bathe or shower, YOU. As a nasty pong, it rates just above baby sick but lingers twice as long.

Wherever you decide to keep your walking money-pit; be it indoors or out, it will get dirty. And remember, this is not just dust and cobwebs we are talking about here. In a stable it will think nothing of lying in its own most recent manure pile (incidentally making it much more difficult to pick up said pile on a pitchfork without it breaking up and spreading even further or getting as much straw and hay entangled in its tail as possible. Turned out in a field, it will roll in the wettest, muddiest patch in winter and the driest dust bowl in summer, and will indulge in this revolting habit as frequently as it can. Horses in the wild do this sort of thing in an attempt to keep their coats free of parasites, but the domesticated horse's reasons can only be described as suspect. Unlike children, who can occasionally be persuaded to wash themselves, when your putrid pony has managed to get himself thoroughly plastered in mud and dirt he will expect you to clean him. Even cats and dogs will lick themselves clean, but not your mucky mare or grotty gelding (I won't mention stallions; you'd have to have less brains than a horse to buy one of them!). They want you to do it all for them. Animal psychologists will tell you that grooming is a very important part of the horse's social life and in the wild herd they indulge in mutual grooming, often standing head to tail whilst nibbling at each others' coats to keep them clean. Watch them in captivity for long enough, though, and you will soon realise that it is as if they are actually enjoying watching you work.

Next to mucking out, grooming has to be the hardest and most thankless task you can perform. You will develop bulging biceps to put Arnold Schwarzenegger in the shade from the constant brushing; your back will ache from the bending to pick out your horse's hooves and your feet will be constantly bruised from where he has placed his great plates on your delicate tootsies on a regular basis. Do not be fooled into thinking that this latter deed is an accident, either. Remember I earlier referred to the horse's eyes being on the side of its head to detect predators? Well he now uses his sideways vision to keep a constant eye on you. He knows exactly where your feet are at all times and it is his equine equivalent of a joke to make sure he never misses. What is more, once he has made contact, he won't get off. In fact, he is more likely to try to lift his other three feet up so his entire weight is on your mangled metatarsals. If he can then turn round a bit and grind your foot even further into the ground, so much the better.

When picking his hooves out, he will lean on you until

If he can lift his other three feet off the floor at the same time so much the better!

you feel like Atlas, holding up the weight of the world on your shoulders.

Your devoted efforts will be entirely in vain, because when you have finished all this brushing and titivating, when you have cleaned his disgusting stable from top to bottom and stood back to admire your labours, or delight in how beautiful your trusty steed looks, it is then time to put him back in his home. The first thing he will do is produce another manure pile and the second will be to lie in it!

For the LOWMS, at this point it is worth considering whether you will have time for all this horsey housework before you go to your own nine-to-five job every day. Apart from the fact that you will be worn out before you even get there, your boss may not take too kindly to you being constantly late, dressed in smelly wellies or reeking of 'Morning Fresh Muck Heap'.

As fathers tend to be the breadwinners in most families, unless Mum is working too (which she may very well have to, in order to keep the children clothed and fed) she will be the one left holding the pony. Still, not much new in that, is there?

And all that work has to be done day in, day out, 365 days of the year. A 'lie-in' is unheard of, holidays become as rare as rocking horse droppings (unless you can find some other poor deluded devotee to take the beast on for a while) and besides, you can't afford one because spare cash is non-existent. Still, you may be wealthy enough to overcome these problems – I believe some people will do anything if the money is good enough – and decide to go ahead and actually look at some prospective mounts. So, what to look for – and what to avoid like the plague?

The first thing you will notice about your future purchase is its size. Let us not be under any misapprehensions about

18

this: bigger is not necessarily better, and there is a good drop of poison in a small bottle! A horse's personality can make the difference or between ownership being merely difficult or totally unbearable, and the size of a particular animal can often have some bearing on their character. Bigger horses cost more to feed, need more space and produce bigger piles of manure. They do, however, tend to be more stupid and less wilful. The little ones are more crafty, wicked and bloody-minded. These are only general observations and should not be regarded as infallible; there are a lot of stupid little ponies and just as many crafty big horses. The difference with the crafty big horses, though, is that they tend to be more philosophical when caught getting into mischief, whereas stupid little ponies just get vindictive.

How can you tell when these dumb animals are feeling philosophical or vindictive, you may well ask. Easy; you can see it in their faces. You can! Horses' faces do not have the same range of expression that humans do, but the eyes and the angle of the ears can speak volumes. The face of a crafty big horse, when he eventually notices you observing his latest misdemeanour with less than adoration in your eyes (which in itself may take some time), will have an 'OK Guv, fair cop' look all over it, while the small pony will have a murderous 'You just wait, I'll get you back for spoiling all my fun' gleam in his eyes, whether he is crafty or stupid. The stupid horse will have no expression whatsoever on his face, except perhaps total confusion, because he is too daft to realise he has done anything wrong and most certainly won't cotton on to the fact that he's been caught.

Big horses have a larger body area to keep clean but are more likely to stand reasonably still while you do it, unlike small ponies who will fidget incessantly and find it highly amusing to nip you playfully (or should that be 'painfully'?) whenever you are in striking range.

After size, the next thing you should look at is the horse's overall conformation. Try to avoid horses that look like something Dr Frankenstein threw together, as these will undoubtedly suffer from more physical problems in later life. Apart from the fact that they are likely to get laughed out of the field by the other horses, your child will not wish to have his or her street cred ruined by being seen on anything less than the perfect equine specimen. Look for a horse that appears to be in reasonable proportion, with all the relevant bits in the right places and without too many lumps and bumps on it's legs. Make sure that it's neck appears to be on the right way up and remember that, whilst big ears may look fine on a donkey, ones that are too large and floppy will do nothing to enhance the air of intelligence one would hope for in the mature horse.

Reluctant parents are advised here to buy their child a pony that is just fractionally too small for them. That way it will be outgrown quite quickly, by which time the novelty will have worn off, the opposite sex will start to look more interesting and they won't want another one. At least boy-friends or girlfriends go home to their own parents once in a while. However, do make sure that the girl/boyfriend doesn't like horses as well or you could be in very deep trouble.

LOWMS must be made to realise that if they do decide to become horse owners, unless they meet another horse owner, they are very unlikely to become parents. They will have neither the time, money or required romantic aroma. Still not convinced? OK, let's look at what your horse is going to eat.

Bigger horses eat more and are likely to be far more fastidious about what they will deign to put in their mouths. All feedstuffs need to be of the highest quality for our equine Egon Ronays and, by that very definition, therefore twice as expensive.

The Equine Egon Ronay

There is no more a disheartening sight than your dear dustbin on legs turning it's fussy little nose up at the equally good, but obviously not so tasty, cheaper stuff and then proceeding to wolf the expensive variety down its gullet so fast it barely touches the sides, not tasting a single morsel of it anyway!

Oats form the main concentrated part of the horse's diet, while it's bulk and fibre come from extortionately-priced hay. Current trends of feeding, however, lean towards the use of ready-mixed feeds which contain all the essential ingredients to keep your horse healthy and you skint. They do, however, have the advantage of being already prepared, which cuts out the necessity for you to weigh and measure several different feedstuffs every meal time. Simply buy the kind that is most appropriate to your horse's lifestyle and follow the manufacturer's guidelines on the bag. It is no good buying cheap feeds for two reasons:

a. Egon won't eat it

and

b. If he is a culinary slob and does eat it, it is highly probable that it will make him ill and therefore cost even more in vet's bills.

There are occasions when some expensive foods are not merely desirable for your horse's health but also absolutely essential for yours. Oats are very high in protein and, as such, give your horse energy. Now, whilst this is necessary for him to keep living and breathing, in some cases it simply makes him too energetic to be of any practical use to anyone. The most well behaved, docile creature can become a totally uncontrollable demon when fed just a few mouthfuls of oats. They start to leap around like they have got dynamite up their rear ends and become the very incarnation of the devil himself. You would be safer alligator-wrestling than trying to ride one of these (see earlier comments about boa constrictors). If your horse is of this type, either sell it to some other poor mug or feed it anything but oats. I believe barley can make them nicely plump and a fat horse will find it harder to leap around without risking a heart attack.

Horses in the wild will graze for anything up to 16 hours a day and not eating will leave them feeling hungry and bored. Feeding plenty of hay will keep him reasonably satisfied and less likely to want to start eating human flesh (or his bed, his buckets, his door, etc.). However, if you are particularly wealthy, there are some excellent alternatives to hay on the market. These consist of specially treated hay and sometimes straw, mixed with molasses or other succulent fruits or vegetables then sealed into polythene bales. They are moist (and therefore twice as heavy as a bale of hay) and supposedly more palatable for your horse. The main drawback though, is you don't need to feed so much of them and are thereby depriving your horse of something to do with his jaws. But if he won't eat good old expensive hay, I would be inclined to dump him before you go bankrupt. He'll want gold buckets next!

Under no circumstances should you feed oats to a child's pony (unless he or she happens to be a particularly nasty little brat who could do with taking down a peg or two and is very well insured). Ponies will eat almost anything and (as the old joke says) are particularly fond of children. These adorably sweet, cuddly creatures, be they the clever or stupid variety, really are the only animals on earth to make vultures look choosy. They will eat till they are ill! They will give themselves colic and laminitis time after time and have even been known to kill themselves by eating poisonous plants such as ragwort or acorns. They just don't know when to stop, but will hate you with a passion if you try to restrict their food intake.

Still, a pony has its advantages in the feeding stakes because it can often do quite well on poorer pasture which will cost you less, in the summer at least. As long as there are a few scrubby tufts of something in the field they will be as happy as pigs in the proverbial. Farmers are always on the look out for someone to off-load their useless patches of land onto and can usually offer you a good deal. Ponies will still need that expensive hay during the winter though, and perhaps some of those nice, pricey pony cubes if they are actually going to do any work. You could always make the kids work during the summer holidays to earn enough to see their pony through the winter, although the NSPCC might not see this as a viable option.

Do ensure that the field you choose does not have any lush vegetation growing just the other side of the fence. This is an open invitation to your pony to brush up on his Houdini act, and he will do this with a dedication to make a nun look like an atheist.

One other small consideration when choosing a field is the water supply. Constant fresh water must be available. If there is no tap, water trough or running stream in the field, here is another chance for you to improve your weight-lifting skills because you will have to carry gallons of water to the field daily – in buckets.

The storage of any pony cubes you may need has to be taken extremely seriously indeed. It may be of benefit to get a security adviser from the Bank of England to check that they are very, very securely locked up. Your main worry should not be that rats or mice will get at them but that they could all disappear at one sitting if your pony manages to find his way into them! Did I forget to mention rats and mice? Oh dear. Well, you may be lucky and only have one or two, but to be on the safe side I would try to negotiate a contract with Rentokil.

The next drain on your bank account comes when your horse or pony becomes ill. It actually starts even before that, because you should never buy any animal without the vet giving it a clean bill of health. This is a privelege that you pay for, not the person offering the horse for sale, so before even thinking about looking for your future purchase, go and pay a visit to your local Vet. If he lives in a huge mansion and drives a Range Rover, give him a wide berth. Look for the one who lives in a council semi and rides round on a bicycle; his charges obviously aren't quite

The next drain on your bank account comes when your horse is ill!

so high. (Either that or he is saving for a retirement home in Monaco, and MRCVS stands for Monaco Retirement Comes Very Steep).

It is only fair to warn you at this point that horses are never trivially ill. When they are poorly it is always something life-threatening or crippling that takes weeks and vast sums of money to cure. You can more or less guarantee that any leg injury will involve months of rest and will occur just before that big show you have been working towards for ages, or the Pony Club Camp, which will render your child inconsolable.

There is no such thing as a simple cough or cold in the equine medical repertoire, it is Chronic Obstructive Pulmonary Disease or Equine Influenza. Nothing minor like chicken pox or measles will affect your four-legged friend. Oh no, they get ring worm mange and other such delightful lurgies, some of which can also affect humans. And whatever their complaint, it will involve every bit as much nursing care as you would devote to your own offspring, but cost an awful lot more to treat; NHS does not stand for National Horse Service. Heaven forbid if your horse needs x-rays or surgery – you may need to take out a second (or even third) mortgage on your house, providing you haven't already had to sell it to pay your feed bill.

Insurance for your animal is something best not skimped on, although, like cars, it is often cheaper to pay for any minor repairs yourself than to lose your no-claims bonus. Premiums range from reasonable for a child's pony that is not going to be doing a great deal, to absolutely ridiculous for any animal that you may wish to compete on, breed from, or keep until it is more than 16 years old.

Are you still there, reader, or have you seen the light and gone hang gliding? I believe parents can find the telephone number of a good adoption agency in the Yellow Pages if needs must.

If you are still reading, either because you are genuinely interested or simply have nothing better to do, I am afraid it just gets worse from here on in. Having looked at some of the horse's welfare costs and problems, it is now time to consider what is required in terms of equipment. You will obviously need buckets for food and water, pitchforks, shovels and brooms for mucking out, and these items themselves are not cheap. A good investment is a prescription season ticket for your supply of Valium, but did you know that both your child and your horse will require clothing? For the child (or yourself if you are a LOWMS) you will need a hard hat. This is an essential piece of equipment if you do not want your head to become as useless as your horse's. There are some interesting designs currently coming onto the market but, whatever style you choose, make sure that it conforms to British Safety Standards and replace it whenever it has a serious bashing (if you feed your horse oats, this could be as often as once a week). A body protector is a must for children and not a bad idea for adults either.

On the footwear front, jodhpur boots are best for children as they allow more freedom of movement of the leg and flexibility in the ankle, with long riding boots being more appropriate for grown-ups for exactly the opposite reason! Good boots can hide a multitude of sins. Never wear training shoes for riding. That is just adding one more danger to an already very dicey pastime, as they can get caught up in the stirrup irons when you fall off. Far better to part company cleanly from your mount than be dragged along by your leg. Long boots can be made of either rubber or leather and the nice rubber ones are quite a lot cheaper than those horrible expensive leather ones.

You will need several pairs of jodhpurs as they get dirty very quickly and often need repairing. Adults, please, regardless of what you may have seen John Wayne doing, do not ride in jeans. Your backside will be sore enough as it is without having the insides of your legs rubbed raw by the seams. Remember, John Wayne had one of those nice, well padded, armchair-like western saddles to protect his seat. Besides, they tend to restrict your movement and you never know when you might need to get your leg over a little bit quicker than normal. Jeans do have their place in the stable yard, though, as they are made of very tough material and can occasionally offer some protection against careless teeth. Again, there is a very wide choice of jodhpurs available. You can now buy almost any colour you want and many come with added extras such as suede knee patches or a 'sticky seat'. There is also a range of ladies' jodhpurs that look nice and slim but stretch to fit almost any size!

A recent addition to the equestrian clothing market is specialist underwear. Thermal longjohns to go under jodhpurs, support briefs for men and, at last, padded knickers for ladies, are now available for the more serious riders to spend yet more of their hard-earned cash on.

For riding in bad weather, the good old waxed jacket is hard to beat, but there are all sorts of ingenious coats to keep both rider and tack dry. The prices vary enormously depending on what name is currently in fashion, but if you or your child are planning on competing you will also need a proper riding jacket. These cost an arm and a leg, so it is worth looking for a secondhand one – particularly for children, as they grow out of them at an alarming rate. There are always plenty on the market as, once people have 'seen the light' and got rid of their overdraft maker, they usually try to recoup some of their losses by selling off their surplus equipment. Tweed hacking jackets look nicest on children as they tend not to show the dirt so much. Adults look best in black or navy blue unless their horse is a dangerous oat eater, in which case they should try the tweed.

Having kitted out the rider, it is now time to look at the clothing the horse needs. In order to be able to ride your horse, you need a saddle and bridle. Bridles are easy, they are completely adjustable and can be altered to fit any odd shaped head you may have acquired and come in all sorts of trendy designs. Make sure that the one you choose is made of steel-reinforced leather as you do not want any parts snapping just as you are trying to apply the brakes. The bit should also be made of steel and there are several varieties to choose from, far too many to go into individually. Most horses will be reasonably controllable in a simple snaffle; some ponies on the other hand will require much more elaborate ironmongery in their mouths to prevent them from decamping whenever they see fit. Get expert advice on this matter, preferably with a written guarantee so you have got someone to sue when Alice's or Oliver's pony runs them under a double-decker bus.

Your main problem, and not necessarily a financial one this time, will be finding a saddle to fit your animal. This may *become* a financial problem if you have to have your saddle made to measure but, generally speaking, your hardest task is going to be coping with your headache. I have seen grown men tearing their hair out at the frustration of trying to get a saddle to fit a small round pony and women screaming in exasperation when the only saddle that fits their mount is too small for their own bottoms to fit in! Again seek expert advice, buy the best quality you can afford and don't be surprised when your horse gains weight six months later and you are right back at square one.

The next items on your shopping list are rugs. No, not the nice Persian ones for the living room floor, but a wide assortment of coverings for your horse's body. Perhaps I should explain here that if your horse is stabled through the winter and you expect him to do any work, he will need to be clipped. Clipping is a task that should only be undertaken by an experienced person or a certified lunatic, as it involves shaving all the horse's natural hair off with an enormous pair of industrial clippers. Now, hold on, I know that to some of you this may sound a ridiculous thing to do when dear old Mother Nature has already provided him with a nice thick, woolly coat to protect him against the winter chills but, you see, he can't actually do any hard work with all that hair.

Unlike humans, who can take a coat or jumper off if they get too hot whilst exercising, the horse cannot shed it's coat for an hour each day and then re-grow it before bedtime. So the normal process is to rid him of his natural covering and replace it with blankets and rugs which can be removed when he occasionally needs to be prodded into a bit of keep fit. Even if he is living in a field all year round, he will still need his belly and chest clipped to prevent him from sweating profusely whilst working. This is particularly applicable to little fat children's ponies who will usually be expected to do a spot of overtime during the Christmas holidays.

For the fully clipped horse, living in a stable, you will need a day rug, a night rug, several blankets to go underneath these rugs when the weather is very cold and a New Zealand rug if he is to go out in a field for a few hours each day. A New Zealand rug is also necessary for the partially-clipped horse or pony living out. For those of you who have never heard of a New Zealand rug, it is basically a large piece of waterproof tent canvas lined with a bit of blanket; you will probably spend as much time cleaning it as you will your horse – it will get every bit as muddy. In fact, if you are that keen on tents, why not get one of them instead? Camping is infinitely more fun, and that is from someone who has suffered a freezing night in a sleeping bag on a stony hillside at an angle of 45°!

So, there we are. Add to this a various assortment of bandages and boots, all specially designed for the elegant equine to protect him from injury whilst either working or travelling and your basic shopping list is complete.

Before sighing with relief or throwing your calculator

out of the window, though, there is one other small item to be added. Although it is not an item of clothing, I have deliberately saved this until near the end so that you have read at least half of this book without ripping it up in disgust. Having a horse is all very well if you are going to keep it in one spot or only ever take it to places that are within walking distance. But if you actually want to take it to shows and the like, you will need some form of transport for it. Two pairs of roller skates and a tow rope will not suffice; you will need a horsebox or trailer.

The good news on this front, and therefore probably the only piece of good news in the entire book, is that you can hire these as and when they are needed, rather than forking out a fortune for something that may only get used half a dozen times a year. There now, doesn't that make you feel better?

There are, of course, countless other accessories that you can buy if you happen to have an understanding bank manager but, parents, do beware that your child doesn't talk you into buying any new fashionable gadgets for their four-legged status symbol. I'm sure that you don't need me to tell you that most fashion trends die out as quickly as they came in and the next one costs even more. For the sake of

Two pairs of roller skates and a tow rope will not suffice!

argument, LOWMS are considered here to be old enough to decide for themselves how to fritter away their hard earned cash on the latest craze.

And so, with pound signs rolling round in our eyes like something out of a Walt Disney cartoon, we stumble to the end of this first section. If you are being relentlessly tormented by a child, or are simply a raving masochist and still considering joining the loony fringe of equine owners – read on!

PART TWO

A ROUND OF FENCES, SEVERAL ROUNDS OF DRINKS

In Part One I gave you warnings about the financial and logistical (not to mention health and welfare) problems involved in horse keeping – be it for you or your children. For those of you who have chosen to ignore those warnings, or are still unconvinced of their truth, I now intend to take a look at the social side of equestrianism and a few of its impending pot-holes and idiosyncracies.

At some stage, unless you happen to have a few marbles left and love your four-legged friend simply as a pet, you may decide that you wish to be a little more involved in the competition side of things. For parents, this will be decided for you by the local branch of every child's mentor – The Pony Club. I wish it to be made clear that I personally have nothing against the Pony Club. Indeed, I believe that the men and women of that organisation do a wonderful job keeping ponies off the street and, once a year, an even better job when they also take the children on Pony Club Camp for a week. However, there is one slight drawback; they like the parents to get involved too. They will run 'Working Rallies' which will inevitably mean you working and, whilst this is fine if you have any knowledge of, or interest in, your child's pet trouble maker, you may need to be on your guard if you are anything less than an equine egg-head.

There may well be several parents at each rally who know virtually nothing of the dark masonic-like world of horses and you can spot these quite easily. They are the group in the corner lamenting the day they failed to persuade their offspring to take up hang gliding, or are simply discussing the weather for want of something better to talk about. They are the ones not wearing the obligatory waxed jackets and green wellies, but are turning their noses up at the smell of a large group of quadrupeds all attempting to put Fisons out of business in one go.

These, however, are the bravest of the brave, men and women who know no fear, for they have courageously stood their ground in the face of some of the most frightening people in the land – the Pony Club Instructors.

The majority of instructors are female and would have reduced any Amazonian woman to a subservient, gibbering wreck in seconds. They will overwhelm the mothers, charm the fathers and intimidate all other non-riding members of the family into helping with the myriad of tasks that are needed to ensure the smooth running of a working rally or (and beware of this one) local gymkhana. The rallies are not necessarily too arduous, but the gymkhanas are a killer. Do you fancy running the tea stall, acting as a steward or perhaps building fences? Any and all of these unpaid jobs are available for the weaker willed, unsuspecting members of the parental public.

Before all you Pony Club instructors who are reading this out of curiosity or boredom go running to your lawyers screaming 'libel', I should like to point out that I once helped the Pony Club as an instructor. Although I am normally a quiet, unassuming sort of person, once I donned my 'Instructor' badge I, too, became an awesome figure to deal with. Hard to believe, I know, but those badges are better than any potion Dr Jekyll might ever have dreamed up and without them, readers, I can state quite categorically that your average Pony Club instructors are usually nice, caring, sensitive people who, like me, often started out as one of the weaker-willed parents.

However, back to the gymkhana. Here, not only do you have to deal with four-legged demons but you will also witness the sort of behaviour usually reserved for dictators or revolutionaries, displayed by the very people on whom the whole of the future of the civilised world depends – the children.

These innocents in pigtails, angels in shorts, little cherubs who are normally their parents' pride and joy will, under the cut-throat pressure of competition, become horrendous, terrifying monsters. They will blame the opposition for everything from their saddle slipping ('Mary must have loosened my girth') to their pony becoming lame ('John kicked Dobbin, he did, I saw him'). No one, including you – dear parent, will escape the acid pouring off their tongue and everyone will be at fault for everything if they don't win every event. There will, of course, be one person who is entirely blameless during these outbursts and that is, yes, you've guessed it, the child in question. If, however, you are cruel and tactless enough to point this out, said child will cry. Not just a gentle sobbing; oh no, nothing so tame. There will be wailing and screaming, foot stamping and throwing (objects first, followed by themselves, onto the floor). A child who doesn't win will make Adolf Hitler look like Mother Theresa. You, if you get roped in to be a steward, will have to deal with not only your own child's devilish behaviour, but also that of several other equally upset children. This in turn can lead to much more serious disputes between the adults, as the little darlings will not hesitate to go screaming to Mummy and Daddy that someone else's mummy or daddy has been picking on them. See how easy it could be to start World War Three? Just have an International Gymkhana and there would be no need for nuclear weapons. Little Alice or Oliver can be equally odious if they win. They will take great pride in mocking the ones who didn't, and you would be amazed at the adult phrases that will issue forth from the mouths of babes. Things like, 'If you taught it to jump properly, you might win now and again' or 'Your parents really should have brought you something more compatible with your ability'.

You, as a parent, and to set a good example to your offspring, must rise above the bickering and squabbling in a way that will have scouts from the Diplomatic Corps knocking at your door. You must rehearse your warmest smile for the smug parent of the winning child. The phrases 'Spoilt Brat' or 'Snobby*! *!' must not escape your lips in public and most certainly not in front of your child, as they are apt to repeat things like parrots. Learning to hold your tongue is often more important than learning to hold your horses.

Running the tea stall can be just as exciting. You will be responsible for offering a great deal of sympathy along with the tea and if you keep a supply of asprins and gin behind the counter you will be guaranteed a job for life. You will be courted by all and sundry, who will want to know what your last customer was saying about the previous customer, or indeed the next customer! Again, you will need to be like the Three Wise Monkeys – hear all, see all and say nothing. Try not to admonish any children for not saying please or thank you (or any adults for that matter). If you can keep smiling and keep quiet, you will be rewarded with one of

*Children on ponies are likely to
knock down an awful lot of fences.*

the best vantage points for seeing all the disputes and disappointments at first hand.

Try to avoid the job of fence building, particularly if you are not terribly fit or strong, unless you fancy yet another chance to improve your weight-lifting. Children on ponies are likely to knock down an awful lot of fences and those poles are HEAVY.

It is also more or less guaranteed that the fences they demolish will be at opposite ends of the arena, so you will spend a lot of time sprinting back and forth. The best piece of advice I can offer here is to leave this job to someone else's teenage son, who will be eternally grateful to you for getting him away from all the idolising teenage girls.

Your own child will also expect you to do a great deal of work on their behalf, cleaning tack and pony before the gymkhana, fetching and carrying buckets of water during the day and spending countless hours holding onto the delightful animal while the child goes off to get an ice cream or hold post-race comparisons with several other children who were not placed.

At the end of the day, whatever the results, the parents must be objective and consoling, encouraging and complimentary. Remember that whatever sort of crummy day you may have had, your child's will have been twice as testing and they will be twice as tired. They will not want to hear you saying 'Never again' or 'That pony is DOGMEAT'. They will want to fall into bed to dream of riding in the Prince Phillip Cup at Wembley or being picked for the England Three-Day Event Team, while you spend the rest of the evening cleaning tack, making sure the pony has eaten his supper, is settled happily for the night, and that all the dirty clothing from the day's activities is whirling round nicely in the washing machine. You could also lay money on the fact that, despite being the last into bed, you will be the first and probably only one to get up in the morning because both child and pony will be either ill or too tired. Still, these are the double delights of being both a parent and a horse owner.

Things do not improve that greatly at the adult level of competition, either. Adults tend to specialise in their favourite aspect of equestrianism such as dressage, show jumping or eventing. Unless you are one of the lucky ones who can afford to buy your horse to suit your sport, you will need to consider first what your dear donkey is capable of. For example, in a dressage arena you would not wish to make a laughing stock of either yourself or your horse by riding a clodhopping animal that looks like its day job is pulling a milk float.

Dressage is art. It is the unification of man and horse in a dazzling display of suppleness and elegance. Getting that message through to the horse is another matter entirely. Many dressage riders advocate the practice of keeping an inspirational vision in mind to help create an overall aura of elegance during the test. However, the beauty in your mind of a painting by Van Gogh or a sweeping melody by Mozart will probably be translated into something indescribable by Picasso or Johnny Rotten in the horse brain and the opportunities for monumental blunders abound. When things go wrong (as they almost certainly will) do not panic. There is only one spectacle worse than a child throwing a tantrum and that is an adult throwing one. It is simply not done in front of the dressage-watching public – well it is, but it really should be against the law. Good manners and good sportsmanship should be the highest priority of anyone who enters into this most graceful but demanding sport. Remember the children are watching; if they see you acting like a child it will not encourage them to act like adults, I can assure you.

The other great advantage of adult competition is that alongside the tea stall there is very often a beer tent. Alcohol is great for helping you to forget, but dressage riders should avoid intoxicating liquor at all costs before their test or they will need double the quantity after to help them forget the test they forgot. You may think that a quick one before entering the arena will help steady your nerves, but judges are not impressed by drunken leers when you are supposed to be saluting them. Also remember to check very carefully before the event what both you and your mount can and cannot wear. To have just ridden the finest test you and your artistic accomplice have ever performed only to be disqualified because you had a sheepskin cover on your saddle to protect your nether regions, is a situation seen only too often and can result in severe depression for weeks afterwards. You will not be able to forgive yourself, and your horse, in his disappointment, will most certainly neither forgive nor forget. Give yourself and your horse the best possible chance of success by making sure you know your test inside out. Walk it yourself before asking Dobbin to participate, so that at least one of you knows where they are going to start with. Practise as much as possible at home so that you can hopefully avoid too many botches on the day. And do remember to look clean and tidy for the actual event. It would be such a shame to spoil a brilliant test because the judges thought you were supposed to be entering the fancy dress competition as Worzel Gummidge and had wandered into the arena by mistake. Create an overall impression of someone who at least looks like they know what they are doing and the judges may just look on you a little more favourably. Post-competition soirées can be very serious affairs where the pros and cons of certain schooling methods (both for horses and children) can be discussed in a refined atmosphere. No getting plastered here; one must conduct oneself with all the dignity and grace one would use during competition. If you want to be a bit rowdier after your chosen sport, why not try show jumping?

Show jumping is definitely not art. There is no need here to be stylish or precise. All that matters is that you and your friend scramble over as many of the fences as possible without knocking them down. If you manage that in the preliminary round, don't pat yourself on the back too soon because you then have to do it all again in the jump-off, but this time at speed. It is one thing to be accurate and another to be fast, but to be fast *and* accurate is something that very few partnerships can manage consistently. Here a 'quick one' before your first round can be a definite asset, as it sometimes encourages the recklessness often needed in this discipline. It can also help lessen any pain you may suffer when your horse refuses to jump, but you aren't given the option and carry on sailing over the poles! In fact, your horse may also appreciate one or two before hand, to assist him in coming to terms with the size of the fences you are asking him to jump. I swear I have actually seen grown horses close their eyes and pray during some rounds and fall on their knees in grateful thanks afterwards (either that or their legs must have turned to jelly in the sheer relief of having got round).

Your dress for show jumping need not be as immaculate as that of the dressage rider, but your headgear is infinitely more important. If you want to wear a motorcycle crash helmet, go ahead. Don't worry that people may laugh at you; it is not their head that is likely to be smashed into the ground at high speed. Your horse need not look too elegant either. He is not there to win a beauty contest and all that matters is that he can jump. Do not be too surprised, though, if he jumps like a stag at home and an elephant at the show. This is a very common phenomenon and you will often hear people moaning that they can't understand what went wrong because Dobbin never tries to put in a short stride before the fences at home. Of course he doesn't; at home the fences are built to suit his stride. On the course, the strides of a wide variety of odd length animals have to be taken into consideration and the course builders are not going to alter the distances between fences for every competitor just because your Dobbin lollops along like a giraffe. People who indulge in show jumping, and often their horses, tend to be much more spirited and forceful, and consequently their post-show parties tend to be much

*Please, Please, PLEASE,
let me get over this one!*

more entertaining and intoxicating than those of the dressage riders. They are far less serious affairs, as show jumpers are more likely to accept that things go wrong sometimes, and that you can't win them all and must just look forward to the next time. So, if you are a party animal, try to persuade your horse that show jumping is fun. This will be much easier if you happen to own one of those excitable oat eaters.

Eventing, which combines the seriousness of dressage, the recklessness of show jumping and the total lunacy of cross country, can only at best be described as an illness. It takes a very special type of person to indulge in this torture, one who preferably had a frontal lobotomy at a very early age. I am sorry if this offends any eventers who may be reading this but, come on, who but a total madman (or woman) wants to charge round the countryside jumping enormous barriers which will not move if you hit them? Yes, agreed they need the artistry of the dressage rider and the courage of the show jumper and should be commended for that. But they must surely only have half a brain, which they then proceed to throw over solid brick walls and down ten-feet drops at breakneck speeds, hoping that their bodies and horses follow suit! And what of the horses? What sort of deranged beasts must they be for going along with this dangerous plan? Is there a home for mentally ill horses where the event riders get them from? Perhaps they, like their owners, have had brain surgery, or maybe they have lost the will to live and are trying to end it all in spectacular fashion!

In this sport, the correct dress is almost irrelevant and the protective clothing inadequate. A body protector, in a serious fall, will do little more than keep the body together and make it easier to scrape off the floor afterwards. All the boots and bandages in the world are not going to offer the horse much in the way of protection either, when he somersaults over a fence and lands on his head (the rider underneath can sometimes make a nice soft landing cushion, though). For eventing, several large 'quick ones' before the cross country stage are not just desirable, they should be

The sound of weeping can often be heard from many a horsebox!

compulsory for both horse and rider. At an event, be it over three days or just one, no one minds very much if the riders are not always polite or are occasionally seen throwing their teddy in the corner. Screaming and obscene language are readily understood by fellow competitors and a few of the spectators, too. The pitiful sound of weeping and wailing can be heard from the back of many a horsebox – and that's just the horses.

Parents should, if they get the chance, take a walk through the competitors' area at a three-day event. It will make a Pony Club show look like a Sunday School outing. Post-three-day event booze-ups are purely a celebration of the fact that the riders are alive and at least physically unscathed. Their mental traumas can only be guessed at, but I have heard rumours that many psychiatrists will be able to afford to retire early due to the increasing popularity of this sport.

Another equestrian activity which, although not officially competitive, can result in some very serious one-upmanship being displayed, is hunting. Now, whatever your personal feelings on blood sports, reader, please try to save some sympathy for the poor unfortunates who indulge in this pointless pastime. These people are sick and need help. They do not have the artistry or recklessness of the eventer, just the madness without the competitive edge. (Mind you, some eventer's hunt as a means of relaxation in between competition seasons). Hunting, however, is a much more social occasion and can even be followed on foot by non-riders, as those nice people from the anti-blood sports league will tell you. There is much more etiquette involved on the hunting scene, from the drinking of the stirrup cup at the meet to the rider's place in the field behind the Master. Dress is also very important, as huntsmen are not given over to wearing the latest coloured jodhpurs or psychedelic hat silks and take great pride in their traditional Hunting Pink. It is ironic to think that a lot of the country's finest businessmen and noblest families all lose their marbles at the same time during the winter. They charge round the countryside, true three-day event style, often in the freezing cold and wet, in order to chase a small mammal the same size as the horse used to be! Heaven help us all if the fox grows by the same scale as the horse in the next million years.

I am not here to make judgements on the rights or wrongs of hunting; each person must square their own conscience with their choice. My concern is for the mental welfare of those who willingly put their lives and limbs at risk and actually join in. *You* may think that you can jump that huge hedge or ditch, but can you actually rely on your horse's confidence that he can do it? That is where the true danger lies – horses are so unpredictable. Who really knows what goes on in those minuscule minds? What may have seemed a small, inviting log to jump last week could suddenly become an enormous, horse-eating monster tree, hiding any number of terrifying nasties this time. You, as the rider, will not be privy to which decision the horse has taken until the very last second. And people do this for FUN?! The fun starts when the horses (and the children) have gone to bed. The annual Hunt Ball encourages many people to take an interest in something that they would otherwise avoid like the Black Death and is usually a glittering social function with men in dinner jackets and ladies in ball gowns. This is the side of equestrianism that anyone can enjoy without actually having to like horses – a bit like supporting the local Rugby club without having to put your body through the mangle of a match every week. Much more civilised and, of course, if you are not horsey you will have the advantage of not reeking of Eau de Cheval!

Carriage driving is another of those equestrian sports that provides more fun for the spectators than the competitors and is a great opportunity to have a good giggle at other people's misfortunes. Some of the antics that carriage drivers get up to would be hilariously funny if they weren't so potentially tragic. The horse has enough trouble lugging its own body behind it without having a great big lumbering cart tagged on behind that. Worse still, some of these people actually lash four or six horses together at a time and then try to negotiate an obstacle such as a river crossing without bridges. They also have their own version of a three-day event, would you believe? Here, the horse or horses perform a dressage test, a cross country phase and an obstacle course. The dressage is performed complete with carriage, so any sudden stops can be a bit risky! The cross country phase is timed, and the obstacles along its path are such that they would be best only attempted in a four-wheel drive Land-Rover, which is where all the fun is.

To watch some of the teams attempting certain obstacles, one has to wonder just what it was they thought they were going to achieve by taking that particular route through it. The final obstacle course involves navigating round some cones without knocking the little balls off the top and reversing in and out of some carefuly laid out barriers. Here the show jumping problem of the course being laid out for all comers can create a few tricky moments for some, that coupled with the fact that some competitors are obviously unsure just how long and wide their vehicle actually is. Still, in their favour it has to be said that carriage drivers at least have the sense not to be on top of one of the lethal beasts. I have to confess that I have only ever personally known one driving enthusiast and although she may have been as mad as a hatter away from her sport, she did at least give the impression of being fairly sane and cautious whilst indulging in her passion and sensibly brought a nice steady type of horse that never got so much as a sniff of oats.

Racing is another equestrian sport where much more fun can be had by not competing, which is often way out of the financial reach of Mr and Mrs Joe Public. Becoming a jockey is a possibility if you are short, don't like food much and are willing to spend years slogging your guts out as an apprentice before getting the chance to ride in the Derby. Being an amateur jockey allows you to earn a normal living whilst riding in races, but the professionals are likely to regard you with slight disfavour. Either you are good enough to turn professional or you shouldn't be riding at all, unless you only ride in races designed for amateurs and don't try to steal their thunder by beating them at their own game. Flat racing is ideal (for those who are small enough) if you enjoy a good gallop but do not wish to risk your neck over fences at 30 miles an hour. But if you are a bit bigger and can't do the weight required for the flat, the jumping game may be your only option. Owning a race horse can be great fun if you can afford:

A. The horse. Thoroughbreds sell for slightly more than the cost of your average six-bedroomed mansion.

B. The training fees. These are about the same as sending your child to Eton.

or

C. The parties at the racecourse. One has to have a supply of the very best champers on ice just in case your donkey wins.

Most sensible parents will realise that finding a budding Shergar at a price anywhere near that of a child's pony is about as likely as finding snow in the Sahara, so encouraging the little dears in this direction is not recommended. My advice is to just enjoy being a spectator, enjoy the champagne on a trip to Ascot and keep your shirt very firmly on your back.

In more general terms, whatever your chosen sport, horses and ponies play havoc with your social life. Apart from the smell which I mentioned earlier, if you are a working owner you will be too tired to go out in the evenings. Weekends will taken up with fence and field maintenance or more shows and gymkhanas; the family will never be fed on time because you will be at the stable or field checking that His Nibs' dietary needs are catered for and any evening when you do manage to escape will undoubtedly be interrupted by an escaped pony or a horse with colic. Romance is tricky, again because of the time factor – you won't have any. It is difficult to feel romantic when you are wearing smelly wellies and are covered in straw, or worse! Parents will be exhausted, juggling caring for the pony and the child, but should be consoled by the fact that they will probably have neither the time nor the inclination to have any more children. Children will not escape unscathed either, as school will become an unnecessary interference with their riding time and their only friends will be other horsey children (until hopefully the novelty wears off).

The final question that has to be asked is, 'Is it worth all the hassle?' Well, if I tell you that I have wished for my own pony over every birthday cake since I was seven years old, have ridden other people's horses all my life and now have a ten-year-old daughter nagging me the way I used to nag my parents, the answer has to be, 'Unless you try it, you won't find out'. I can say however, that I am now 30-something and for the last 20 years I have had people telling me all the things that I have just told you. I have had to make do with riding school ponies, friends' horses or any other old donkey I could lay my hands on – and I feel deprived.

So I think I might just give in to my darling offspring, totally disregard my own advice, go and grovel to my bank manager and warn my lawyer (and my husband) that a divorce might be on the horizon!

GLOSSARY

LET'S
SPEAK HORSE

Aids, Artificial: These are the items used to assist with the Natural Aids (below) and include whips, spurs and martingales. (See separate entries).

Aids, Natural: The technical term used for the signals given to the horse to get him to do what you want him to do. These can range from the almost imperceptible nudges with the leg and the gentle piano playing action of the fingers of the dressage rider, to the blatantly obvious boot in the ribs and ham-fisted tugs of the darling child on the fat pony.

Bandages: To protect your horse from knocks and strains – very handy for human use too.

Barley: A good feedstuff for horses who get hyperactive on oats – makes them nicely plump.

Biting:	A nasty habit that many horses develop to relieve you of your fingers.
Bits:	The piece of metal that goes in the horse's mouth and enables you to stop and steer the beast. Size and severity depends on what type of hard-mouthed lunatic you have ended up with.
Bolting:	There are two definitions of this word:

1. Eating too quickly – likely to give the pig colic.

2. Running off uncontrollably with you on board – liable to give you an upset stomach

Boots:	These come in various designs and, like bandages, protect various parts of your horse's anatomy from injury. It is advisable to have steel toe caps in yours.
Bran:	A feed that looks a bit like fine sawdust and adds bulk to a horse's diet (and waistline).
Bridle:	A collection of leather straps that fit round the horse's head and hold the bit firmly in the animal's mouth.
Bridle, bitless:	A collection of leather straps that fit round the horse's head without the added advantage of having a nice chunk of metal in the strategic place.

Brushing:	This is where the horse bangs one leg against the other as it is moving, usually either because its legs are too close together or it is too lazy to pick its feet up properly.
Bucking:	A nasty habit that many horses are prone to, whereby they leap into the air in an attempt to get you off their backs – usually successfully.
Canter:	The third fastest pace after walk and trot. Feels a bit like being on a boat on a rough sea.
Clipping:	The removal of the horse's coat in winter, necessitating the purchase of expensive rugs to keep him warm. (Also useful round the ears of certain children.)
Colic:	Equine belly-ache. Usually caused by the horse being a pig or eating something it shouldn't.
Colt:	A male foal. Trouble from day one until gelded (see separate entry).
Conformation:	The overall way the horse looks, or rather should look.
Cross Country:	A highly dangerous equestrian sport enjoyed most by those with a total disregard for their own safety.

Dock: The nice word for a not so nice part of the horse's anatomy, just under its tail.

Doer: A term used to describe how the horse thrives. A good doer will get fat on next to nothing and a bad doer will always look like an equine Biafran no matter how much high quality expensive food you cram down its throat.

Doubt: What you should be feeling now at the prospect of owning a horse.

Dressage: The art of getting the horse to move correctly, obediently and willingly. Easier said than done.

Eventing: A three-stage equestrian sport consisting of dressage, cross country and show jumping. Suitable only for the more dedicated masochist.

Exercise: Plenty of exercise is needed for the stabled horse to prevent him from climbing the walls.

Eyes: A good guide to the horse's character. When buying a horse, try to find one whose eyes aren't crossed or have an evil gleam in them.

Farrier: The very brave man who puts shoes on your horse. Not to be confused with a blacksmith, who is the man who could make you a very nice wrought iron gate.

Filly: A female foal. A much better option than a colt.

Fresh: A term used to describe the horse that is feeling full of the joys of spring and consequently leaping around like a demented head case.

Gallop: The fastest of the four paces. Guaranteed to terrify the living daylights out of anyone doing it for the first time and very often on subsequent attempts.

Gelding:
1. An adult male horse that has been gelded.

2. Castrating the male horse. This makes them much more controllable and less embarrassing around female horses. A lot could be learnt here in the human stakes. Best done when the horse is young before it realises what it might be missing.

Green: A term applied to the young horse who hasn't yet learned how to carry itself or behave properly. Can be applied to some older ones too.

Grey: A horse of any colour between almost white and dark lead. Impossible to keep clean.

Hand:	The unit of measurement used for horses and ponies. One hand is equal to four inches, but 15 hands sounds less intimidating than 60 inches – that's five feet!
Hay:	A very expensive name for dried grass.
Haynet:	A large string bag to put hay in to keep it off the ground. Essential unless you want a lot of your expensive hay trodden into the muck.
Horse:	Any equine over 14.2 hands high (four feet, ten inches) in his stocking feet.
Incisors:	The very large and very dangerous teeth at the front of the horse's mouth.
Injuries:	These are very common in the equestrian world and you should always have the phone number of your vet and local hospital ready.
Jockey:	A small person who rides races on large horses for fun or money.
Jockey Club:	The governing body of racing who try to bring order out of potential chaos.
Jumping:	The art of getting an animal who wasn't designed for the purpose to leap over fences that he probably can't see very well without knocking them down.

Kicking: Yet another nasty habit that many horses will indulge in, often for no good reason and with remarkable accuracy.

Kimblewick: A type of bit that can offer a fairly effective braking system for many a small pony.

Knees: The middle joint of the front legs only. Do not show your ignorance by referring to the 'back knees', these are called hocks.

Knees, Broken: Do not have a heart attack if your vet tells you your horse has got broken knees. Broken refers to the skin over the knee, not the bones.

Lameness: There are many causes of lameness, all of which will leave your horse limping and unable to work. All injuries will require the services of a vet to sort them out and will generally cost you an arm and a leg.

Lungeing: A method of exercising either young horses or a horse who for some reason cannot be ridden. It involves you standing in the middle of a circle while the horse runs round you attached to a long rope (lunge rein). It can make you very dizzy but has the added advantage of your being able to carry a very large lungeing whip to fend off the beast if he gets fed up and decides to charge at you.

Mare: An adult female horse. Mares have been known to show the same PMT-type symptoms as human females, so do try to make allowances for their hormones if you buy one.

Martingales: Known as an artificial aid, these very useful items consist of a series of leather straps that attach to the saddle and bridle to prevent the horse from raising its head above the angle of control or from throwing its head up and hitting you in the face. I personally think they are most effective when they allow no more than a couple of inches of movement in either direction.

Money: Although not strictly an equestrian term, everything equestrian eventually boils down to it.

Mucking Out: The general term used to describe the act of cleaning out a horse's stable. A back-breaking, thankless task best left to someone else if possible.

Napping: Although this may conjure up comforting visions of your dear Dobbin having a peaceful snooze, it is actually the term used to describe general misbehaviour and cussedness.

Neckstrap: A leather strap (often an old stirrup leather) placed round the horse's neck for the rider to cling on to in case of emergencies. An essential piece of equipment for the novice rider and very useful for the more experienced ones, too.

Nuts: Can be applied to the horse's mental condition but generally means the small pellets of feedstuff given to ponies.

Oats: The main ingredient of the stabled horse's diet but likely to make some horses too lively to be safe to ride. Should never be given to small ponies as it will turn them into monsters.

Overfacing: This is the term used for asking the horse to jump fences that are too big, too soon, too often, resulting in failure. Like most of us, if horses keep getting things wrong, through no fault of their own, they are apt to give up.

Overreaching: This is an injury inflicted on the back of the front hooves by the front of the back hooves because the dumb beast is too slovenly to put its feet in the right place.

Pelham: A type of bit that is good for strong horses and ponies with the added advantage of being able to have two reins fitted to it, offering double the leverage of a single rein.

Pony: Any equine under 14.2 hands high. Smaller than a horse but no less dangerous for it.

Puissance: A jumping competition in which a large wall is raised by several inches each time, until only one horse is left. The equine equivalent of the high jump.

Quality: All feedstuffs must be of the highest quality and in this context it means expensive.

Quidding: This is when the horse drops half-eaten food from its mouth when it is eating. If children did this we would make them leave the table but if a horse does it, it means yet more cash for the vet.

Rearing: Of all the horse's nasty habits, this has to be the most dangerous. This is where the horse tries its human impersonation and stands up on its hind legs so you fall off backwards. To add injury to injury he will occasionally fall on top of you as well.

Ringworm: A delightful parasitic skin disease that your darling horse will think nothing of passing on to you.

Roller: No, not the motor car. This is a wide webbing belt to keep the horse's rug on. Anticast rollers have a metal arch at the top so the horse can't roll over and risk getting his legs trapped against the wall. Horses regularly do this because they are so stupid they very often can't see a huge brick wall right next to them.

Rugs: These range from light cotton sheets to heavy duty waterproof coverings for your horse. The manufacturers know that the likelihood of you being able to make your own is pretty slim and consequently charge the earth for them. The word monopoly springs to mind.

Saddle: The seat that goes on the horse's back. Undoubtedly invented by a man to prevent his assets being stripped by the horse's backbone. Until recently they were made only of leather but are now available in synthetic materials. This breakthrough in modern technology doesn't necessarily make them any cheaper, though.

Spurs: Known as an artificial aid, these are little metal spikes which the rider attaches to his boot to persuade the horse to go forward with just a little bit more oomph!

Stable: A horse's home. Will definitely not apply to your financial condition.

Stallion: An adult male horse that has not been gelded. Unless you are planning on breeding from them, stallions are best avoided like the plague. They are big, powerful bullies who, like a lot of men, only have one thing on their minds. Bearing in mind the minute size of the horse's brain, this leaves no room for him to think about anything else.

Sweat Rug: Horse's string vest.

Temperament: Refers to the horse's general character and behaviour. Can mean anything from slightly mentally unbalanced to vicious psychopath.

Tendons: A band of tough tissue that attaches the muscle to the bone. In a horse's leg these sustain injuries with the regularity of grazes on a child's knee but are infinitely more difficult to treat. Your vet will be laughing all the way to the bank when your horse has a tendon injury.

Trailer: A horsebox towed by a car (as opposed to a complete lorry). Although usually cheaper than a lorry and less heavy to insure, it will mean replacing the family car more often on account of the rear axle dropping off.

Trot:

The second fastest pace, where the horse springs from one diagonal pair of legs to the other. A very bouncy pace and, when first tried, the rider may have the feeling of being shaken until his teeth rattle. As the rider progresses they will learn to do the rising trot in which they stand up and down in the stirrups in time with the rhythm of the pace and thereby lessen the concussion to their brain.

Twitch:

A barbaric device which can be attached to either the horse's ear or, more usually, top lip and is then progressively tightened until the animal has no choice but to stand still. However, if you have a horse that can be very difficult to clip or shoe, or tries to eat the vet (hence putting up his charges), I can supply the pattern for a homemade one for a small fee.

Unsound:

A polite way of saying hopping lame or three-legged.

Valium:

A strong tranquiliser that you may find very useful in moments of equine-induced stress.

Vice:

Any one of the nasty habits (bucking, biting, rearing etc.) previously described, plus any number of other vicious or disgusting traits displayed by our equine friends.

Walk: The slowest of the four paces. A nice steady pace in which one can cover long distances in reasonable comfort, so why bother going any faster and putting your health at risk?

Whip: A big stick for (in riding-speak) 'reinforcing the leg aid'. In other words for clonking the brute if he won't move when you ask him.

Whoa: The word used to slow or stop the horse. Often screamed very loudly by many a rider as they are carted off over the horizon.

X-ray: Yes, we all know what an x-ray is, but you get yours on the National Health whereas you have to pay for your horse's. Just pray he never needs one.

Yearling: Exactly as it sounds, this is a colt or filly of one year old. Just to confuse the issue, though, a thoroughbred race horse is counted as being one year old until the second January the 1st following its birth. Simple isn't it?

Yielding, Leg: Leg yielding is a sideways movement generally performed at the walk or trot. It is a good suppling exercise but not recommended before your horse can actually walk in a straight line, otherwise he is likely to fall flat on his face.

Zebra: A member of the horse family with black and white stripes, from Africa. Often seen in zoos, which is probably the best place for a great number of our four-legged friends.